Elements of Design

LINE

Elements of Design
LINE

Jack Selleck

Art Teacher, Emerson Junior High School
Los Angeles, California

DAVIS PUBLICATIONS, INC.
Worcester, Massachusetts

To "Bully" for telling me since I was a boy that my art work was good even when it was awful; and to Jane and Ed for being special people.

Title page:

Bold, black lines and the angled, active white lines add a sense of drama and immediacy. *Christ and Judas*, Karl Schmidt-Rottluff, Woodcut 19" x 17", Los Angeles County Museum of Art. Gift of Kurt Wolff

Copyright 1974
Davis Publications, Inc.
Worcester, Massachusetts, U.S.A.

Printed in the United States of America
Library of Congress Catalog Card Number: **74-82679**
ISBN 0-87192-063-8

Type: 10 point Theme Medium
Graphic Design: Thumbnail Associates

Consulting Editors: Gerald F. Brommer, George F. Horn, Sarita R. Rainey

10 9 8 7 6 5 4

CONTENTS

LINE: A Record of Ourselves

Have you ever walked along a dirt road or a sandy beach with a stick in your hand? It is almost impossible not to draw or leave a mark of some kind. Perhaps just a meandering line that follows you or a particular line pattern or design done either subconsciously or by plan.

Much of early man's environment is recorded through line drawings, etchings and paintings. A young child's first art expressions usually emphasize the use of line. We can find examples of line everywhere: in nature, in architecture, in clothing, food, art works and utilitarian objects.

Line is always combined with one or more of the other art elements: FORM, SPACE, TEXTURE, and COLOR. By

becoming aware of line around you, you can gather information for your own art work, whether representational or abstract. What you see and learn and feel about line (structure, strength, delicacy, movement) can help you evaluate and appreciate both your art work and that of others. Line can also be appreciated for its own sake.

In the busy world we live in, it is all too easy to be unaware of the visually exciting things that surround us. If this book helps you to become more conscious of LINE and its infinite possibilities for enjoyment and use, it will have accomplished its goal.

LINE AS STRUCTURE
holding things together

Perhaps you have heard an author discuss the "backbone" of a play, or maybe someone say, "structure your thoughts before you begin", or read that the football team's success was "structured" around a strong running game. In other words structure is the "bones" or strength that holds materials, things or ideas together and makes them weak or strong. A bridge may be safe or collapse because of its structure or lack of it; a painting might look "well put together" or visually "fall apart" because of its structure.

Structural lines can be delicate and thin like a spider's web or thick and bold like the underpinnings of a pier. Sometimes strong and delicate lines are seen together in interesting and exciting combinations. Photo by Britt Phillips

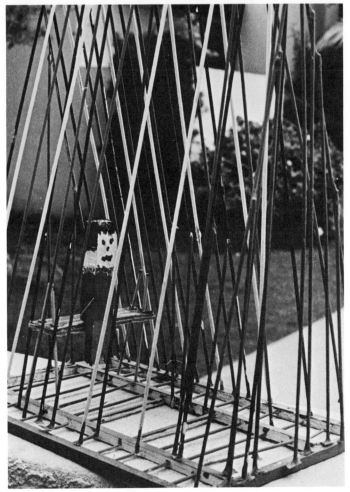

A balsa wood figure sits quietly inside a structure made of applicator sticks. Emerson Junior High student work

The Air Force Academy Chapel provides spectacular examples of structural lines. (interior and exterior)

10

One excellent way to gain an understanding of structure is to observe and understand how trees develop: roots, trunks, branches, twigs, leaves.

This large, fallen tree looks like the skeleton of some prehistoric beast, or perhaps a huge, many-legged insect slowly pulling itself along the ground in a science-fiction movie.

Insects have devoured much of this leaf, but its basic structure remains intact. Note the fascinating irregular line edges which remain. Photo by Walt Selleck

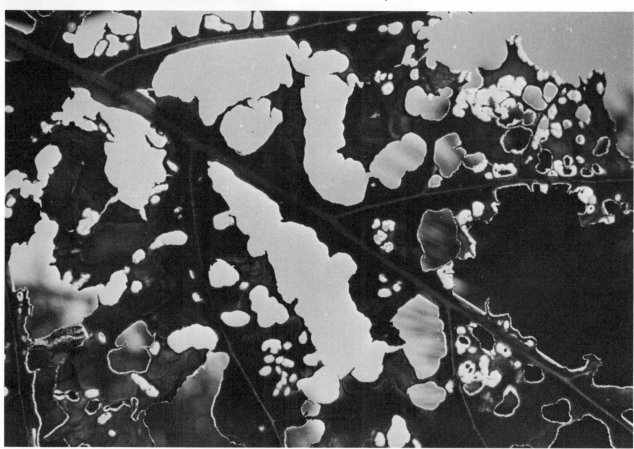

Whether you live in a large city or small town, LINE structure is there to be observed and to challenge your imagination.

The metal "ribs" of this abandoned amusement park turnstile seem unwilling to accept their "forced retirement."

Line structure around town

This rock and gravel plant is like a giant combination of
different sculptural approaches — a comparatively delicate
cone shape sits atop powerful vertical, horizontal and diagonal
lines and moving parts.

Take a careful look the next time you see a house being built.
The structural framework lines are often more interesting than
the finished building.

14

This telephone pole was passed by many times; but, one day just before dusk the silhouetted bold lines of the pole and the medium and fine wire lines formed a dramatic arrangement.

One of the greatest innovative structures, the geodesic form, is used at this playground to climb on. This type of structure can cover a football stadium or, perhaps in the future, a whole city.

Line structure is seen in the rigging of a still active sailing vessel, the skeleton of a prehistoric deer and in the wagon wheels that attempt to help the past remain alive. Skeleton found at San Josecito Cave. Courtesy of the Natural History Museum of Los Angeles County.

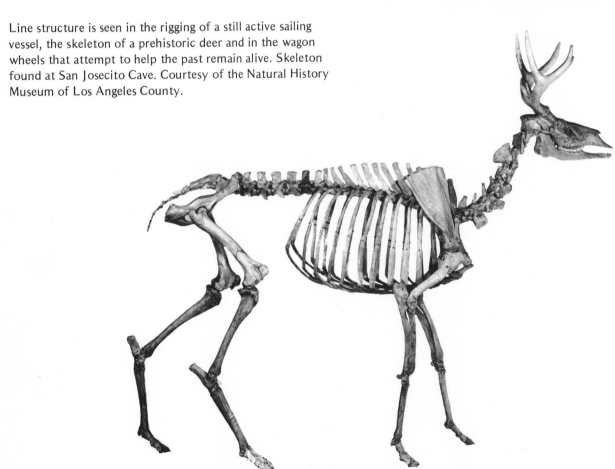

These tall electric light towers are structures built to withstand wind and wear. They can present an eerie sight standing like giant robot sentinels guarding the land. A less romantic eye could justifiably classify them as ugly blemishes on the landscape. A closer look shows the strength and abstract beauty created by the angled lines of metal. Tower photos by Walt Selleck

This small but dramatic abstract structure is made of balsa wood and applicator sticks supporting a suspended plaster form. Emerson Junior High student work

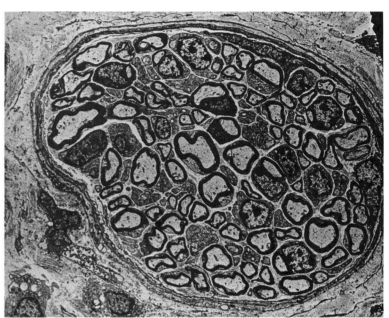

This nerve cell, magnified over 9,000 times, is an example of the intricate structure that exists in nature. Lines describe and portray shapes within the cells, tissues and organs of which we are composed. Photo courtesy of University of Southern California Medical School, Cancer Surveillance Program.

Applicator sticks and India ink on illustration board were used for this structural exercise. Emerson Junior High student work

Powerful brush strokes, some running off the canvas, set up a dynamic structure of bold shapes and lines. *THE BALLANTINE,* Franz Kline, Oil on canvas 72" x 72", Los Angeles County Museum of Art. Estate of David E. Bright

LINE IMPLIED
edges, lighting, meetings, dots

Line can be implied where it does not actually exist. A row of tall trees suggests a line that leads our eyes into the distance.

Our eyes will also fill in the space between a series of dots or marks, thereby creating a line. Edges of objects, shapes or forms, flying sparks in a factory or the repeated water flow of a fountain also imply line.

21

Large forms may appear as lines when viewed from a distance; a freight train rolling across a landscape, members of a marching band or, as seen here, cars lined up during the 1974 gas shortage.

A sunlit line on the left edge and the sweeping roof line emphasize a beautiful "shape of sky" in between.

Line is implied where two shapes or areas of color come together. This fine painting is a good example. *PREMIERE 1957*, Stuart Davis 1894-1964, Oil on Canvas, H. 58" W. 50". Los Angeles County Museum of Art, Art Museum Council Fund

Thousands of light bulbs create a dynamic array of lines and shapes.

The sun trying to fight its way from obscurity lights the edge of a cloud.

An ivy leaf splits apart, leaving a line of emptiness, and the sun-dried cracks in the earth lead to the hoof prints of a horse like a series of tunnels connecting small craters. Hoof print photo by Ann Plauzoles

Nature's implied lines

LINE AS TEXTURE AND PATTERN

Line is seen in nature and man-made objects, describing
texture (rough, smooth, bumpy, etc.) and creating pattern
through repetition.

Backs of chairs and their shadows at an antique store create an interesting line pattern.

Sunlit lattice fills an ordinary patio with a quiet, delicate pattern of light and shadow.

Crisp shadows and crossing lines add up to a visually exciting stairway.

The back of this merry-go-round building is rich with a variety of line, texture and pattern.

Lines on the jacket and in the brick mingle freely with the reflected lines of the building and sidewalk across the way.

Tall Buildings

patterns
windows
angles
lines rising upward
textures
light
reflections
glass
cement, wood, metal
railings
shadows
smooth, rough
patterns
textures

29

A great variety of line can be found in nature — the bark of a tree, the stripes on a zebra; where rain, sand and silt combine and where canyon walls have been formed and etched by the elements and by time.

Photo courtesy Los Angeles Zoo

Ink lines are used over water color to suggest the pattern of the bricks and to define and emphasize other objects and shapes. Emerson Junior High student work

The variety of angled, curved, shallow and deep lines on this plaster carving result in interesting light and shadow patterns and textures. Emerson Junior High student work

This linoleum block carving of a stylized face is rich in line texture and pattern, particularly the hair. Senior high school student work

Lines were etched into the forehead area, the collar design and the legs of this mythological ceramic beast. Emerson Junior High student work

Line, Texture and Pattern in Student Artwork

LINE TO USE

You speak into the telephone and your voice travels over lines . . .
You wear a vertically lined shirt and look slimmer . . .
You might like the looks of a chair or a car because of its "lines" . . .

A beach playground area horse waits patiently for another potential rider. The metal lines serve the purpose of climbing and also describe the structure of the animal.

A student guitarist finds a secluded spot during the lunch hour. The guitar, of course, has metal strings (lines), but also a unique, contour line shape.

A belt can be thought of as a line and this particular belt is enhanced with an original free-line design carved into the leather. Emerson Junior High student work

Slightly opened Venetian blinds create lines of light and shadow and combine with the window frames in a simple, quiet design. If stared at for a length of time it begins to vibrate visually, similar to an Op Art piece.

The way light falls and reflects on and in objects made of transparent materials emphasizes the outside shapes of the objects, their "lines."

Chairs, plant holders, racks . . . lines of wrought iron shaped for many uses.

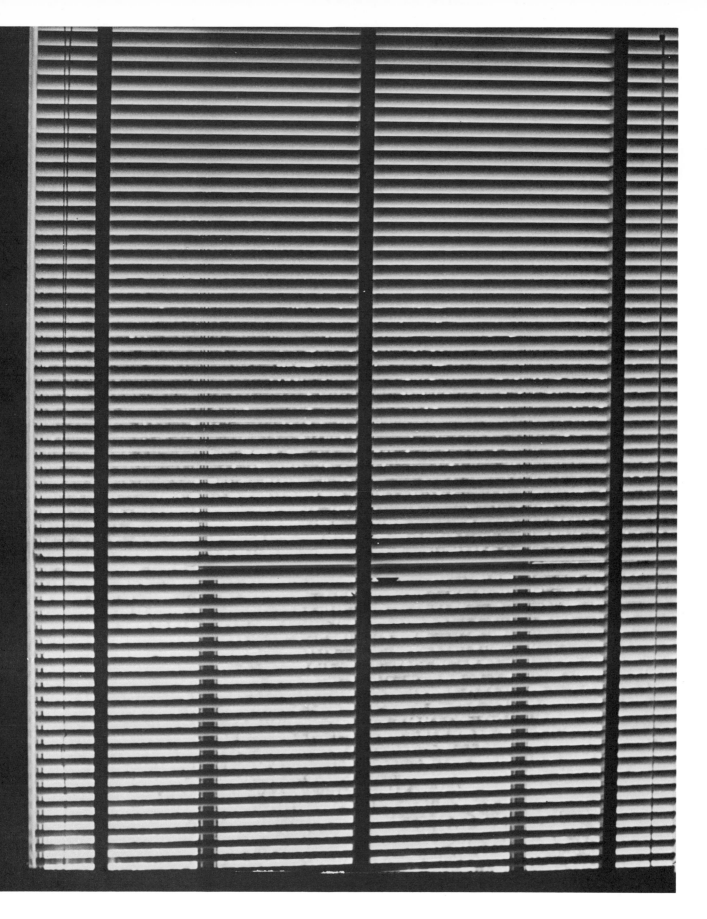

LINE WITH PERSONALITY
direction, mood, movement, expression

Line has direction — it pulls our eye up a tall tree or "jiggles" it as we drive by a picket fence. An artist can direct our eye through his art work by the way he uses line.

Vertical lines remind us of ourselves standing. They also bring other associations to mind; tall buildings, soldiers at attention . . . stability, dignity, tallness. Horizontal lines may suggest the ocean, the horizon, the body at rest . . . calmness, repose, breadth, quiet. Diagonal lines — falling, leaning, growing . . . lines of action, movement, unbalance, drama. Curving lines smoothly sweeping, turning, bending . . . the edge of a cumulus cloud, the rings of a tree trunk, the curling smoke from a chimney.

The interior view of this museum provides a fine example of the strength and dignity of vertical lines.

The upraised arms and the vertical stripes on the referee's shirt add to the exciting moment . . . TOUCHDOWN!

An elongated, vertical sculpture becomes a monumental tribute to the human form. *Tall Figure, 1,* Alberto Giacometti, 1901-1966, H. 106¼", Los Angeles County Museum of Art. Lent by Norton Simon, Inc., Museum of Art

Vertical lines

The quality of a line can reach our emotions and suggest mood; nervous, quick strokes can add a sense of tension or drama to a drawing or painting . . . a firm, smooth line may give us assurance and allow us to calmly view it. Fuzzy, blurred lines may suggest a dreamy, mysterious mood while repeated curving lines alternating from thick to thin might achieve a hypnotic effect, whether in a work of art or formed in the sand by water. Broken, jagged lines might evoke a sense of apprehension, irritability or concern.

The horizon line in the Grand Canyon sunrise is a good example of the quiet and calm suggested by horizontal lines.

Although there are many shapes and objects in this painting (by the author), its basic structure is comprised of three horizontal bands.

40

The architects of Greece stressed horizontal lines to add serenity to the temples of their gods. In a much more modest way the basically horizontal shape of this public library adds to its serene look. Photo by Walt Selleck

Horizontal lines

These two pages have been horizontally designed to help illustrate the less active look when compared with other page layouts.

Poised on their diagonal supports, these amusement park airplanes suggest the movement that will take place even though they are temporarily at rest.

The fan-like sculpture line contrasts beautifully with the quiet, simple lines of the building.

A plant grows, its diagnonal rays reaching towards the sun.

Diagonal lines

This photo was taken the morning after a small clothing shop was burglarized. The jagged line edges of glass remain as a reminder of the act.

43

44

The Bentwood Rocker is based on an 1860 design. The curving lines suggest calm movement and relaxation as a rocker should.

The curved arches of this metal fence seem appropriate surrounding a religious temple. The arches, in an abstract way, seem to echo the shapes of the trees in the background.

Unintentional humor is provided by the attempted sweeping elegance of the lettering, contrasting with the trash cans and typical back alley surroundings.

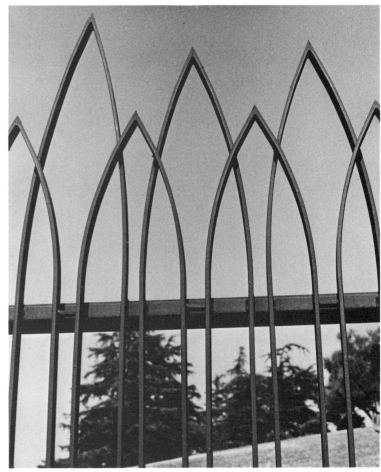

Curving lines

"... drawings are invaluable, not only because they give us in their purity the mental intent of the artist, but because they bring immediately before us the mood of his mind at the moment of creation." Goethe

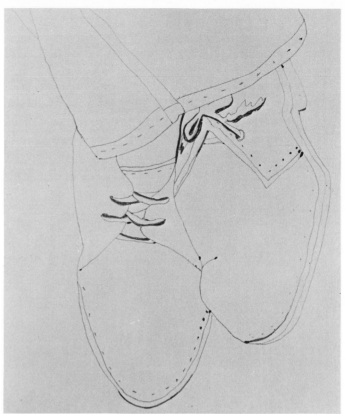

Lines that describe the edges and surfaces of objects are called contour lines. This is one of the most natural ways to draw as seen in this drawing of crossed feet. By a high school student

Sometimes people doodle on a telephone pad or on a piece of scratch paper or, as this student did, on a notebook. This spontaneous act results in a fascinating piece of art reflecting subconcious, unique and personal ideas.

Commercial artists often use a crisp, simple line to make their ideas more readily seen and understood.

Wide, horizontal stripes can make a "chubby" person appear a little "chubbier."

Miró's line is playful and, at the same time, haunting and mysterious in its floating abstract way, while the wire sculpture cat of an Emerson Junior High student is perky and comical. Both works are alive with line personality.

Formes Animées, Jóan Miró (Spanish, 1893-), Oil on canvas 68" x 76½", Los Angeles County Museum of Art. Estate of David E. Bright

Line, mood, and expression

Volcanic ash caused this eerie scene of ghost trees; some fallen, others remaining quietly vertical, the distant trees seem to have been withering when the "end came." Devastation Point in Hawaii. Photo by Paul Wegeman

49

LINE THAT TELLS US WHERE TO GO

Whether taking part in a sports activity, driving a car or just walking along, lines guide us, help us or hinder us, depending on the situation.

This empty parking lot contrasts the narrower car space lines with the short, stocky lines of the cement retainers setting up a visual, almost musical, repetitious beat.

The headlight cover lines, the bright bumper and the parking area lines combine to give the appearance of a strange street version of tick-tack-toe.

The empty tennis court with its boundary lines and white-topped net becomes as elegant and pure as a minimal, hard-edged painting.

This bowling alley's bright, waxed lines invite a roll of the ball.

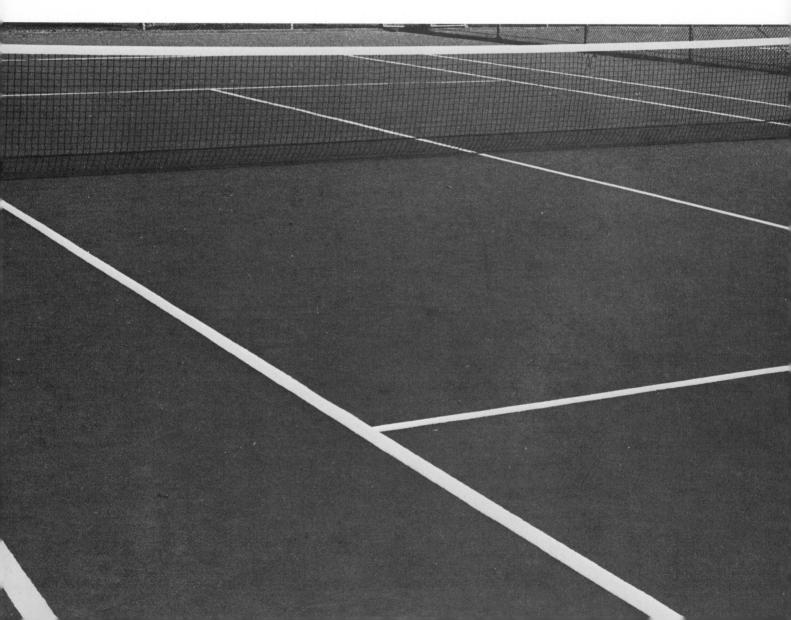

The angles, direction and movement of lines are combined in this oil painting from the Tennis Court Series by Roger Kuntz. Photo — courtesy of the artist

The trees, bridle path railings and shadows evoke a tranquil mood.

LINES . . .
The wide diving board textured line . . . the metal railing
lines . . . lane-lines on the pool's floor . . . the rope retainer
line . . . the lines of the life guard's tower.

The lines in this linoleum block horse race describe the track
rail, the suggestion of the stands and, by being a multiple
print, suggests fast movement as well. Emerson Junior High
student work

Once, trains rumbled over these railroad tracks but now youngsters use them for their games of imagination — "walking the tightrope" or "holding up the train from Dodge City."

55

Whether a quiet path through the woods, an ordinary residential street or a giant freeway system, each has unique line characteristics.

Two oil paintings from Roger Kuntz's Freeway Series. The top painting shows the lane lines and edges moving into the distance and includes details of the scene, while the second painting emphasizes the edge lines of the mass of concrete in a more abstract treatment. Photos — courtesy of the artist

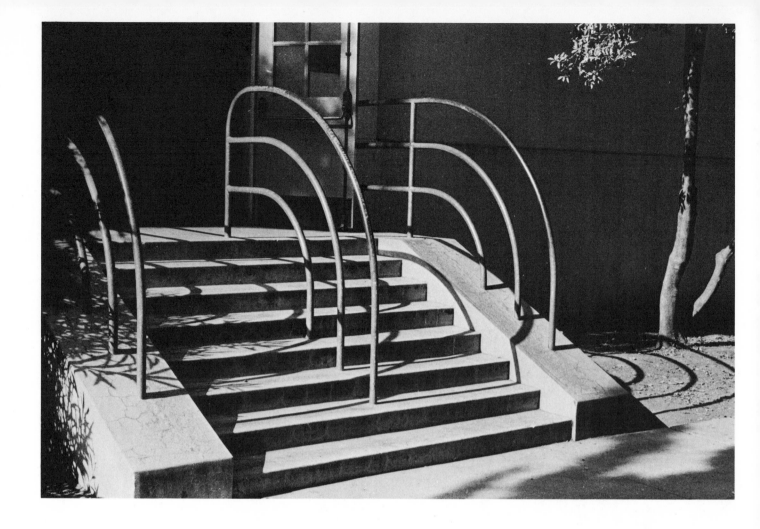

LIN(E)ING UP A SERIES

Many subjects could be used to show how line is readily available to see and enjoy. This section deals with the wealth and variety of line to be found on and around the schools.

Interior and exterior stairways and windows can provide
striking line patterns.

59

The wide line stencil letter shapes were photographed after a fresh painting made the word "school" more noticeable on the street.

Some simple and often unattractive things, when seen in detail and in certain light, can become visually interesting as illustrated by this cracked blacktop in the school parking lot.

The service lines at the Student Store seen in the morning light just before business hours.

A student chalks in some paddle-tennis court lines.

This ordinary fence with a corrugated metal shed in the background was photographed when the shadows were "right" to capture the almost optical illusion effect of space.

The bike rack — Wheels, Spokes and Shadows.

The basket, the chain net and shadow, the edges of the backboard and buildings, the pole . . . many lines seen in a small area.

LINE FROM A DIFFERENT VIEW

Lines in art employing different concepts and materials,
objects photographed from a certain angle or under certain
conditions; things appearing as something other than what
they are; these are some of the ideas offered in this section.

Stained and etched with the effects of time, this canyon wall in Arizona resembles a non-objective painting.

Small, delicate branches in the foreground appear as large as the tree branches farther away. This flattening effect results in an overall free pattern of natural lines somewhat like a controlled drip-technique painting.

This photo of rich and unique bay water reflections reminds one of an abstract painting.

Close-up of a linear sculpture with the museum building lines in the background visually combining as part of the design.

A rusted clothes pole and the clotheslines become serenely beautiful immediately after a rain.

A unique pattern was created by the combination of the heat reflector images and the grille-work of a small portable electric floor heater.

Photographers use many techniques and special effects to convey their message. One of the most common, yet effective, is the combining of two or more photographs into one. This is called superimposing. Photos seen on pages 22, 24, and 28 are superimposed and shown here. Note the dramatic changes that occur.

Computers can be programmed to produce works of art. Photo courtesy of California Computer Products, Inc.

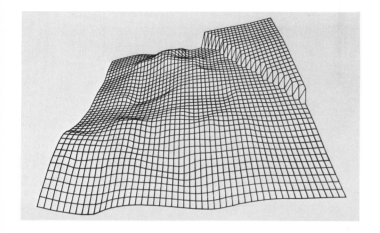

These Mexican-American artists use symbols and graffiti common to the Chicano culture and community to produce a bold, honest, people's art work. Using spray can paint, spontaneous and free felt lines are incorporated in this large mural. *Group Mural, 1973*, Carlos David Almaraz, Gilbert Lujan, Roberto de la Rocha, and Frank Romero; a collective work. Acrylic spray paint on canvas, 12' x 9', Los Angeles County Museum of Art. Los Four

This photo looks as if it might have been shot from the back of a moving amusement park ride or even a rocket. Actually, the sense of movement is caused by the lighting, angle and line direction. What you really see is an angle shot up a ladder inside of a hangar. Photo by Walt Selleck

This large painting uses the thick, bold lines of the protractor shape, interweaving in the center while thinner lines separate shapes and colors in the central area. *Protractor Variation, 1969*, Frank Stella, Fluorescent-alkyd on canvas, 20' x 10'. Los Angeles County Museum of Art

Three similar photos of light reflections in a swimming pool combined as a triptych, a technique that is used by some painters.

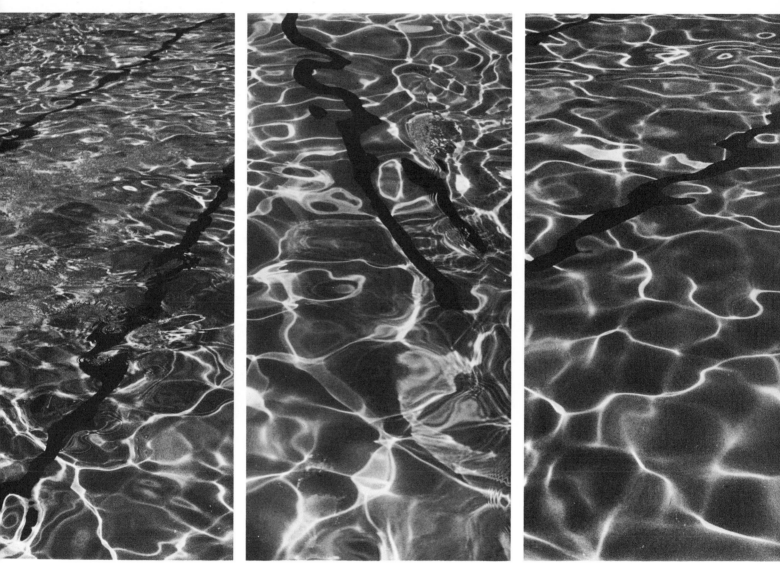

Notice the beautiful variety of shapes within the line divisions.
This non-objective painting quietly celebrates the visual joy of
line as our eyes follow its journey across and off the canvas.
Hard Edge Line Painting, Lorser Feitelson, Enamel on Canvas,
60" x 72", Los Angeles County Museum of Art. Anonymous
Gift

These delicate and elegant nature lines are actually a parasitic growth that attacks new shoots and plants.

Below: Argon, helium — neon laser beams, and mirrors were used to create this 100-foot, L-shaped corridor environment. *Day Passage,* Rockne Krebs. Executed in collaboration with Hewlett-Packard Corp. for the Art and Technology Exhibition. Los Angeles County Museum of Art, May 10 — August 29, 1971.

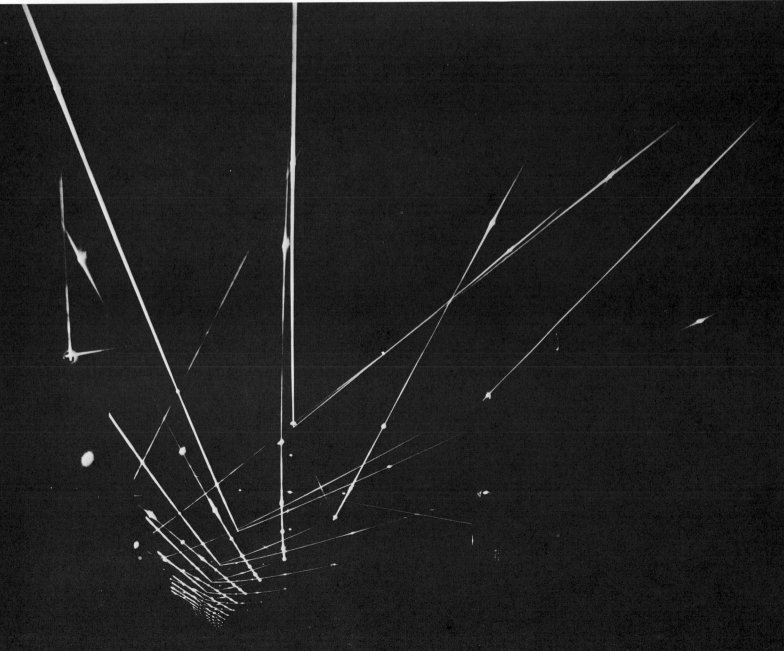

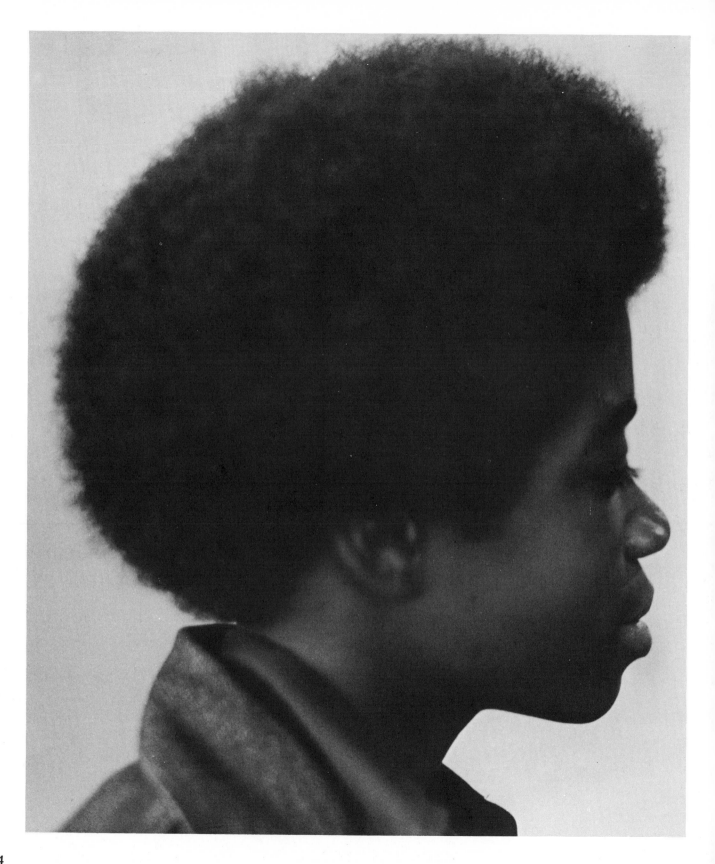

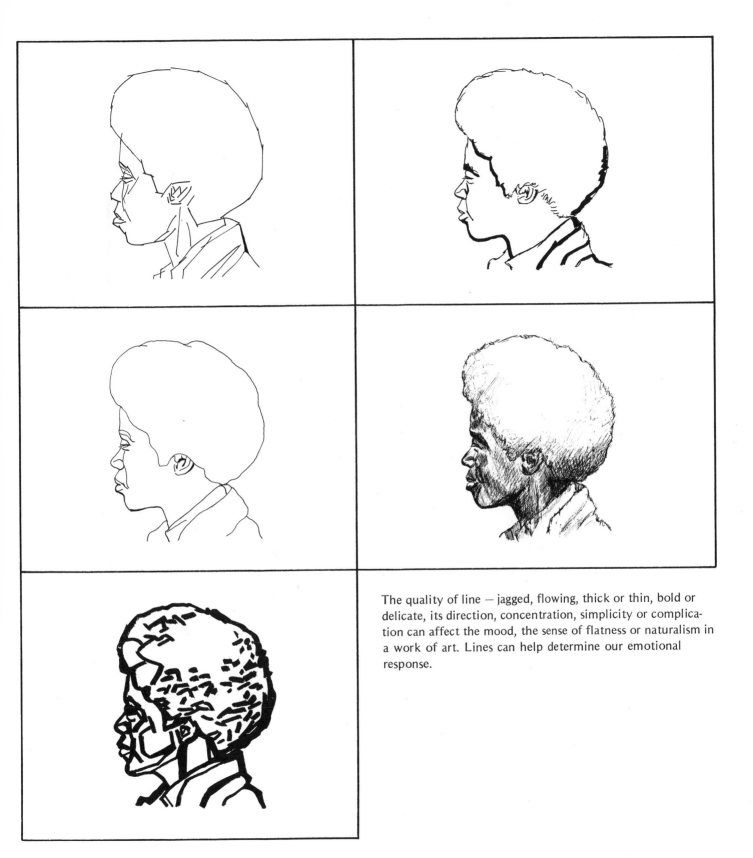

The quality of line — jagged, flowing, thick or thin, bold or delicate, its direction, concentration, simplicity or complication can affect the mood, the sense of flatness or naturalism in a work of art. Lines can help determine our emotional response.

All photographs in this book were taken by the author unless otherwise acknowledged.

76

POPLARS AT GIVERNY, Claude Monet, French, 1840-1926, Oil on Canvas, Los Angeles County Museum of Art. The Jones Foundation of Los Angeles

Lines and trees

Stylized straight line tree study — felt markers on illustration board. Adult school student work

INDEX